HAGAR

In the Face of Rejection, God Says I'm *Significant*

STUDY GUIDE | FOUR SESSIONS

Kasey Van Norman, Jada Edwards,
Nicole Johnson

With Karen Lee-Thorp

ZONDERVAN

Known by Name: Hagar

This title is also available as a Zondervan ebook.

Requests for information should be addressed to:
Zondervan, *3900 Sparks Dr. SE, Grand Rapids, Michigan 49546*

ISBN 978-0-310-09645-0

Cover image: © LanaBrest/Shutterstock
Interior design: Denise Froehlich

First Printing November 2018 / Printed in the United States of America

Contents

How This Study Works

Hagar: Overlooked? Not Invisible.

Hagar was manipulated and betrayed by people in authority over her. People she trusted to know what was best. How would you respond in that situation? Hagar first lashed out and then ran away. Her story invites us to look at our own lives and ask, "What hurts have propelled me into shame and hiding from others or from God? Where am I paralyzed by a fear of rejection? What experiences have led me to question whether I matter in this world? Do I recoil at the idea of forgiving certain people? When it feels like things will never be okay again, is God still there? Does he even see me?"

Hagar's story doesn't wrap up with a neat bow. We are left not knowing what happened to her. Her story teaches us that we don't always get to see the happy ending, but the unresolved things in our lives compel us to trust the God who knows the ending and is at work for our good.

Hagar: In the Face of Rejection, God Says I'm Significant is a study for women who want to get into the real, messy parts of our lives that are usually under wraps. Through each video session, we will engage with a Bible teacher, a Christian counselor, and an actor portraying present-day scenarios. These leaders will help us explore the human perspective of Hagar: how she felt, how she saw herself, and how others saw her, as well as how we see ourselves. We will also discover God's perspective: how God sees Hagar, and how God sees us. Through these perspectives, we will find our own stories in the pages of Scripture.

A session of this study will go like this:

Check In. In Session 1 you'll introduce yourselves. In later sessions you'll have a chance to share something you discovered about yourself in-between the sessions.

At a Glance: Hagar. This is a quick snapshot of an age-old problem we still deal with today, Hagar's age-old solution or mistake, and a taste of God's wisdom on the subject.

Video Notes. Each video segment is 18–28 minutes long. It opens with a drama and then moves into a fast-paced teaching. Session 1 begins with all three of the presenters together, talking about the theme of the series. This study guide contains space for you to take notes on what you see in the video.

Group Discussion. The heart of the study is your conversation with the other women in your group. You'll be talking mainly about the real experiences of your lives. However, because this isn't group therapy, we strongly recommend that you commit yourself to the group ground rules discussed below.

Closing Prayer. End with your group leader or a volunteer reading aloud the prayer suggested in this section. Of course, any offered prayer is acceptable.

Keep This Close. These are a few short, memorable lines from the video that you may want to copy into your phone to go back to during the week.

On Your Own. Finally, you'll find activities you can select from to carry your exploration of the topic deeper during the week. There is one verse of Scripture you can memorize and come back to over the four sessions of the study. There are journaling ideas. You can read Hagar's story in the Bible. You can pray with guided quiet time or reflect on the drama. Do whichever of these activities you find helpful. Don't feel pressure to do more than you have time for. You'll have a chance to share something you got out of these activities when your group gathers next time. You'll also have a chance to recite your memory verse together.

Group Ground Rules

This study gives you more of an opportunity to open up about your real life than most studies. You won't be pushed, but you will be invited, to talk about how you see yourself and how you live. But your group is not a therapy session. It's not led by a counselor. If you need professional counseling or a forum to share the story of your past, ask your group leader or church officials to recommend resources.

The following ground rules will help you stay on track. You should go over them in your first meeting to be sure that everyone understands and agrees.

Confidentiality. Everything shared in the group must stay in the group. Don't repeat to outsiders what others share, even if you are all friends. If a group member misses a meeting, don't bring her up to date by sharing what others said in her absence. If something happens in the group that upsets you, don't discuss it with someone outside your group. Go to your group leader.

Disclosure. This should be a safe place to tell the group the difficult truths of your past. However, the group does not need all the ugly details. Give your group the four-or five-sentence summary of your situation. If you need someone to hear the whole story, ask your group leader to help you get connected with a counselor. She can help you find the person in your church staff who has the names of counselors in your area.

Tears. It's often good to cry when you share something hard. You're not embarrassing the group. If someone in your group cries, avoid words and actions that attempt to fix her sadness or solve her problem. Comfort is good; fixing is not. Don't let tears derail your time together. Keep going. The woman who has tears will be better sooner if the conversation carries on.

Shared Airtime. Everyone in the group needs an equal chance to talk. Avoid telling long stories, especially about your past or about what you are struggling with today. If you have a lot on your mind that needs to be said, ask your group leader to help you get connected with a counselor.

Present Orientation. Hagar's past will come up in the study, and you'll have some time to think about your past. But for group discussion, concentrate on talking about who you are today, shaped by your past, but not living in the past. Don't ask the group to sit through an account of what you went through. That's for counseling.

Advice. Avoid giving advice to other group members. If someone reveals a problem she is having and doesn't seem to know what to do about it, it can be tempting to suggest solutions. Avoid doing this. You can give her the gift of listening to her and accepting her as she is, and you can pray for her later on your own. Likewise, you should avoid asking the group to suggest solutions for situations you are facing. If you feel out of control and need help, ask your group leader to help you find a counselor.

What Materials are Needed for a Successful Group?

- Television monitor or screen
- DVD player
- Four-session DVD
- One study guide for each group member (you will be writing in the study guide, so you will each need a copy)
- Bible(s) (at least one for the group, but encourage all members to bring their Bibles)
- Pen or pencil for each person

SESSION 1

Exposing the Lie of shame

Emotion IN THE **MOMENT** CAN MAKE US **FORGET** THE CONSEQUENCE OF OUR DECISION.

Many of us are on a never-ending quest to counter messages from our world that we are insignificant. Maybe the message of insignificance comes from comparing ourselves to those who have wealth and status, or maybe we compare our perception of beauty. Maybe our idea of insignificance stems from stories of "better" mothers, or others who seem to have a sense of purpose that we lack. We may put enormous effort into a social media presence that says we have life all together and are achieving what we "should" be achieving. Yet in one instant, social media can shatter our security and make us question, "Do I measure up? Should I be doing this the way *she* does?"

In this study we'll be introduced to a woman of the Bible named Hagar, the slave of an insecure and impatient woman named Sarah. (We all have some Sarah in us.) We'll see how both Hagar and Sarah were desperate for significance, mired in the feeling that the world saw them as deficient, and hiding their shame by mistreating others. We'll also discover that we're not doomed to be stuck in patterns like this, because God sees us, he knows us, and he can be the person we run to when the world tells us we don't matter.

Welcome to the first session of *Hagar: In the Face of Rejection, God Says I'm Significant*. To get started, give everyone a chance to do the following:

- Say your name, unless everyone in the group knows you. Then take one minute to tell a little about what your life was like in junior high school.
- Take a minute on your own and write down your response to this question (you won't have to share your answer): on a scale of 0 to 5, how confident are you that you totally belong to God despite your popularity or platform in the world? Mark where you are on the measuring line below.

0	1	2	3	4	5
Not at all confident					Very confident

At a Glance: HAGAR

Age-old problem: Shame over feeling deficient in some way

Age-old mistake: Trying to hide shame by treating someone else like she's deficient

God's timeless wisdom: Run to God for refuge and acceptance. *"But I am not ashamed, for I know whom I have believed, and I am convinced that he is able to guard until that day what has been entrusted to me" (2 Timothy 1:12 ESV).* It is difficult to feel less than or deficient when you first consider Jesus. Think of him first and your whole perspective of self will be righted, the shame the world may be throwing at you will suddenly seem irrational and irrelevant. Jesus stands guard on our behalf and defends our worth.

Video Notes

Play the video segment for Session 1. It's about 20 minutes long, and you will be introduced to three speakers. As you watch, use the following outline to record thoughts that stand out to you.

DRAMA: Nicole

Feeling insignificant can lead to feeling like you don't matter.

Being treated like you are insignificant can lead to feeling like you are invisible.

TEACHING: Jada

Sometimes we are a victim of someone else's choices (parents' addiction, bad relationships, etc.).

Sometimes the emotion of the moment can make us forget the consequences of our decision.

You can love Jesus and still feel like your life is heading in the wrong direction.

TEACHING: *Kasey*

Shame is a feeling that starts with embarrassment, can quickly move to anger, and then to pride.

Shame will always look like hiding.

Remember the question: Does this reinforce, or does this release my shame?

GOD'S not just your hope, he's your *purpose*.

Group Discussion

Leader, read each numbered prompt to the group.

1. What stood out to you most from the video?

2. Hagar was in part a victim of Sarah's and Abraham's choices. *They* chose to stop waiting for God to give them a child. *They* chose to make Hagar the surrogate mother for a child Abraham would have with her, a child they would adopt as their legal heir. She didn't have a say in the matter. What are some ways we today can be victims of someone else's choices?

3. What do you think we can do about being victims of someone else's choices? What can God do?

4 Jada talked about hope. How strong are you in hope right now? What motivates you to have hope? What gets in the way?

5 How do you define shame? What can move us to feel shame today?

Select a volunteer

to read the following:

Shame always leads to hiding in some way. For example, Sarah felt shame over being unable to bear a child. In her culture, bearing children was the number one way women proved their worth to society. Without children, women were often seen as useless. Sarah decided she would hide behind her servant Hagar. Hagar would have a child with Abraham, and society would count it as Sarah's.

Unfortunately for Sarah, Hagar felt shame too. So, when Hagar got pregnant, she decided to hide her shame by tossing words, facial expressions, and body language of contempt at Sarah. Shame and hiding don't always move a person to become a wilting wallflower; they often move a person to lash out at others.

6 What does hiding from shame look like in our behavior today? Give some examples. Think of examples that involve attacking others as well as examples that look meek.

7 Read Hebrews 6:17–20. Instead of hiding in shame, we can flee for refuge to God's inner sanctuary, where Jesus has gone before us. How do you think fleeing for refuge in God is different from hiding in shame behind church or Bible study or spiritual practices?

In preparation for the coming week, write one thing you want to gain from your study time:

(ex: hope for my future, a better understanding of who I am . . .)

Closing Prayer

Ask for a volunteer to read this prayer aloud over the group:

Creator God, thank you that you can bring good out of our suffering when we have been the victims of other people's choices. Thank you that you can even bring good out of our suffering when we have made choices that have landed us in places of forced servitude. We put into your hands all our shame, and all of the ways we hide from you and other people. Please come to us in our places of hiding and lead us out. We want to choose to take refuge in you. Thank you that you fully accept us as we are, in all our messiness. In Jesus' name, amen.

Keep This Close

As you go on your way this week, here are some thoughts from the video that you may want to save in your phone or write on a sticky note so you can refer back to them:

- Even when we feel like victims, in God we are vindicated.
- God fully accepts us. He has set us free from condemnation and shame.
- Instead of hiding from people, we can run to God for refuge.

SESSION 1

On Your Own

Each session of this study also includes activities you can do each day between group meetings. These will help you work through and into a deeper understanding of both the Bible and how it relates to your personal life. **Don't feel you need to do all of these activities. Choose those that are helpful to you. The goal is to grow and develop a stronger relationship with God.** There will be time at the beginning of your next meeting to share whatever you've learned from these activities.

Memory Verse

There are many good techniques that may help you memorize Bible verses. Here are some of them:

1. *Write out the verse by hand on paper, along with its reference (Genesis 16:13). We remember as much as 80% more of what we write by hand than what we type electronically. That's because handwriting stimulates a more helpful part of the brain than typing does.*

2. *Even better, hand write the verse and reference five times.*

3. *Read the verse aloud and act it out in an exaggerated way. Proclaim it dramatically. Actors have learned that the dramatic use of your body and voice will create associations in your brain.*

4. *Go for a walk and recite the verse and reference aloud. Walking increases memory formation.*

5. *Copy the verse and reference into your phone or onto a card you can keep with you.*

6. *Return to the verse three times a day to rehearse it. Say it aloud. Do this for the whole four weeks of this study.*

Learning the verse with its reference will help you find it in the Bible if you want to read the larger story around the verse.

One thing we really hope you'll do is memorize a verse of the Bible. Committing verses to memory enables you to deeply internalize their truth and to have them with you when you need them. Here is the memory verse for this study:

She gave this name to the LORD who spoke to her: "You are the God who sees me."

(Genesis 16:13 NIV)

In this verse, Hagar is coming to multiple conclusions about her past, her present, and ultimately her future. She claims or names God *El Roi*, which means "God sees me." Think about that for a moment. In an instant, Hagar is made aware that she is not only seen, her life mattered and was recognized. Her pain, struggle, insecurity—vindicated at once because God declared that he saw her, he was paying attention, he had her.

In Real Life:

DRAMA ACTIVITY: Enough, Part 1

A former waitress becomes the manager of the diner where she works. She accepts the position because she needs the extra money to support herself and her young daughter. But the job begins to take over her life so that she scarcely sees her daughter anymore. This would be hard enough, but she feels the owners misled her and now treat her as if she doesn't matter.

1. Do you think the character in the story was correct in her assessment of her situation? What informs your belief?

2. What features of your life (if any) send you the message that you don't matter?

3. Are there roles or responsibilities in your life that tell you that you do matter? What are those things? Are there people to whom you matter who let you know this?

4. How would getting the message that you don't matter affect your behavior? For example, if you got that message, what might you do to compensate or to make yourself feel better? How might you try to protect yourself from people? Or how could you hide from them?

5 Read 1 Peter 2:9–10. The apostle Peter wrote to some scattered groups of people from a variety of ethnic backgrounds. He wrote to them about being a chosen race and a royal priesthood. Do you believe deep down that you are part of a group that God has set apart? Would it change anything if you believed this? What would change?

6 What might it take for you to be convinced that God has chosen you?

7 When God picked Abraham to be the head of a chosen family, he didn't do it in order to form an exclusive club for people who could feel like they were better than everybody else. He did it to show Abraham's family what it was like to be blessed *in order that they could then be* a blessing to all the families of the world (Genesis 12:3). Likewise, today when God chooses people from all over the world to be part of his family, he doesn't do it for them to feel like they are better than those around them. He does it to make them a blessing to the world. How does this affect the way you view the idea of being chosen?

Hagar in the Bible

SCRIPTURE ACTIVITY

Look up Genesis 16:1–6 in your Bible and read the story.

God had a long-range plan to rescue human beings from the consequences of their attempts to run their own lives apart from him. He planned to rescue all families by first focusing on one family. That family was going to be the descendants of a Middle Eastern man named Abraham. God had promised Abraham that all the families of the earth would be blessed through him. There was just one problem: Abraham and his wife, Sarah, kept getting older and older, and Sarah never got pregnant.

Our story picks up when Sarah was far past menopause. (At this point, Sarah is called Sarai and Abraham is called Abram. God would change their names later.)

1 In the group discussion, you talked about how Hagar was the victim of other people's choices. On the other hand, what choices did she make herself in verse 4? In verse 6?

2 What do these choices reflect about Hagar?

3 Shame is a feeling of being seen and found deficient. Sarah felt deficient because she was childless. Hagar felt deficient too. Have you ever felt deficient in some way? Do you still feel deficient in any area? If so, why?

4 Shame leads to the desire to hide and not be seen. There are a number of common hiding behaviors. When we hide, we may treat other people with contempt, as if they are worthless or deserve scorn. Or we may treat ourselves with contempt. Would you say Sarah is more inclined to treat herself or other people with contempt? How does she show that? How does Hagar show contempt?

5 What about you? Have you ever treated someone else with contempt, even subtly? If so, what did that look like in your actions or words? Have you ever treated yourself with contempt? If so, what did that look like?

6 What are a couple of tweets or even a Facebook post that Hagar might have made over the course of her pregnancy?

7 What is your takeaway from this study? What do you want to do about it?

Shame and Hiding

TEACHING ACTIVITY

Shame leads to hiding. We can hide behind:

- Our husband, children, or another relationship
- Our status—being considered influential, smart, honorable, respectable, successful, or spiritual
- A job
- Popularity or approval by a certain group
- Our looks or our smile
- Bible knowledge, church volunteering
- Busyness
- Social media

Use your answers to these questions to journal on your own and process through your prayer time.

1. Are you hiding? If so, what are you hiding behind? That is, what do you use to distract people from looking directly at you as you really are?

2. When do you hide? Are there certain people or situations you hide from, or do you hide from everybody all the time?

3. Think of your behaviors and relationships. Which ones reinforce your shame? Which ones make you more aware of your inadequacies? Which ones lead to feelings of condemnation?

4 Think of your behaviors and relationships again. Which ones restore confidence and help to release your shame? Which ones draw you closer, especially on your bad days? Which ones lead you to the truth? Which ones cause in you a longing to change? Which ones convict you without condemning you?

5 What do you want to do differently in your day-to-day life as a result of this reflection?

As a believer, we get to HIDE. We just have to HIDE in the right place.

Journal Time

Choose one of the following topics to journal about:

- Have you ever been the victim of someone else's choices? If so, what was that person's choice? How did it affect you? (For instance, how did it hurt you, cause you shame, help you grow, isolate you, cause you anxiety or fear or some other emotion, or increase your understanding of something?) How did you respond (or how are you responding)? What results came from your response? What do you think would be the best available response to that situation?
- Are you currently in a situation that makes you question if God knows what he's doing? If so, what's going on that prompts that thought? What feelings are you having about your situation? (Get them all out in an uncensored way. Use colored pens if that inspires you.) How did you get here? How have you been trying to manage your feelings and the situation? How is that working? What do you think would be the best way to respond to your situation?
- Have you been mistreated by anyone in authority over you? If so, what happened? What feelings have you had about that? How have you responded in actions and attitudes? What have been the results? Colossians 3:23 says, *"Whatever you do, work heartily as for the Lord and not for man" (ESV).* If God is your purpose, and not success or achievement or fairness, you will be better equipped to deal with mistreatment. How helpful is it for you to think about that? Why? What do you think God wants us to do if we have been abused or if someone at work has crossed the line of harassment?

Whichever topic(s) you choose, finish by answering this question: What do I want to do differently in my day-to-day life as a result of this reflection?

PRAYER ACTIVITY

In our insanely busy world, it's enormously valuable to set aside even a few minutes away from the distractions to think about what God might be trying to get through to you. God speaks to the heart—the core of you, where your thoughts, emotions, desires, motives, and choices come from. He speaks above all through the Bible. He also speaks in other ways, such as through his people. He can speak through circumstances, using them to highlight something he has said in his Word. He doesn't give "new revelation" that contradicts what has been written, but he does guide you in how his words apply to your unique life. Sometimes he is trying to get through to us about a blind spot that others see or about a hard decision we are facing, but we can't hear him over the noise in our lives.

Find a quiet place where you can be alone. Maybe take a walk, sit on the porch, head to the nearest park bench, or simply sit in your car alone for a few minutes. Turn off your phone—or better still, leave it somewhere else so it doesn't draw your eye and your thoughts. Lay before God whatever you have read or heard recently from the Bible. Lay before him any shame you have and any tendency to hide. Offer him your worries. Think of at least three things you have to be thankful for and thank him for those. If there are things people have said to you, or said in your group meeting, that stick in your mind, ask God what he might be saying to you through those. Invite him to put together the pieces of what you need to hear from him. Then see if you can rest in the silence for a few minutes. If you get distracted, gently turn your mind back to your memory verse or one of the things you're thankful for. Don't be discouraged if you don't hear an audible message from God. Just being more open to him is the important thing.

SESSION 2

Rejected to accepted

Hagar was a slave. When Sarah told her to have a child with Abraham, she didn't have the freedom to say no. When she ran away from Sarah, she had nowhere to go if she didn't want to die in the desert. Compared to her, we may have lots of options to say no or go somewhere new and start over.

But despite our external freedoms, we may still experience internal bondage—we may be held captive to a painful memory, unresolved relationship, or, unhealthy habit. Regardless of the presentation, all captivity comes from the same place—the fear of being rejected upon exposure.

What can we do about this fear? In this study, we'll see what Hagar did. We'll discover that transformation starts when we come to believe God's promise that he knows and accepts us fully, even on our worst days. And we'll explore ways of coming to believe this deep down where it counts. We don't have to be in bondage to anything—even fear. God wants to set us free.

Check In

Before you dive into the video, take a few minutes to check in with each other. Let each person choose one of the following to respond to:

- What did you get out of the "On Your Own" practices you did for Session 1?
- When you were a child, what did people around you do when you misbehaved?

Next, say your memory verse aloud together. Be sure to say the verse reference after it. If you don't know the verse from memory yet, read it with the group from page 25.

At a Glance: HAGAR

Age-old problem: Harsh treatment

Age-old mistake: Run away

God's timeless wisdom: Trust that God sees. He sees what you are going through and he is with you. Stay and work for what is right when possible, you are not alone. Running does not get you closer to God, it only delays your reunion. *"'You are the God who sees me,' for she said, 'I have now seen the One who sees me.'" (Genesis 16:13 NIV).*

Play the video segment for Session 2. It's about 20 minutes long. As you watch, use the following outline to record thoughts that stand out to you.

DRAMA: Nicole

Running doesn't resolve what's unresolved inside of us.

TEACHING: Kasey

Freedom is any place in us that believes we are fully and finally accepted in God.

God doesn't want us to make peace with our bondage.

What is wrong? Where in my heart have I gone to get to this place as a Christian?

At the root of our slavery is the fear of rejection.

Satan loves when we withdraw from people.

We can get stuck looking at the "WHAT." But *freedom* is found in the "WHY."

Group Discussion

Leader, read each numbered prompt to the group.

1 What stood out to you most from the video?

2 The drama was about a woman knitting and talking about running away. Do you tend to run away from people and problems? Or do you stay and face them? Give an example.

3 Kasey said, "Freedom is any place in us that believes we are fully and finally accepted in God." What are some of the behaviors of someone who truly believes she is fully accepted by God, even on her worst days?

4 What are some of the behaviors of a person who isn't sure she is fully and finally accepted by God? Try to think of a wide variety of behaviors that might reflect this doubt.

Select a volunteer

to read the following:

God accepts a *person* without approving of all of her *behavior.* God grieves and disciplines all behavior that draws us away from his goodness. He loves and forgives us even on our worst days and in our most destructive behaviors. He demonstrated that when Jesus was arrested and tortured and sent to the cross. As he was dying in that horrific manner, Jesus said of the very people who had crucified him, *"Father, forgive them, for they know not what they do" (Luke 23:34 ESV).*

This can be hard for us to believe if we have had the experience of being rejected because of our behavior. We all have bad days, as children or adults, and people haven't always treated us with love and forgiveness on those days. But we can learn that God is different and that some people are different as well.

5 Describe ways you can recognize when someone accepts you as a person.

6 How does the fear of rejection sabotage meaningful relationships? Think about the behaviors that might flow from a fear of rejection. Then think about how those behaviors affect relationships. List some here.

7 Satan can harass us when we withdraw from others. What does withdrawing look like? Try to think of as many different ways of withdrawing as you can. For instance, how can we withdraw while still being around people? List the ways you withdraw here.

8 When we start thinking in extreme ways, we think in terms of "always" and "never." "I will never be enough. I will always be misunderstood. I can never go back to that church. I will always be alone. I must end this relationship completely because there is no hope of reconciliation." Together, fill in the blanks with other "always" and "never" statements that we might believe.

I will always ____.

I will never ____.

He will always _______________________________________.

He will never ____.

In preparation for the coming week, write one thing you want to gain from your study time:

(ex: hope for my future, a better understanding of who I am . . .)

Closing Prayer

Ask a volunteer to read this prayer over the group:

Father God, in the midst of his suffering, your Son forgave his persecutors for what they did to him. Please help us believe that you accept us on our worst days with our worst behavior. Please help us believe what you say about us in the Bible. Go into the scared, unfree parts of us, and speak your words of acceptance and healing to those places. Thank you for the other women in this group. Let your Holy Spirit go with them as they walk through this week, and keep speaking words of acceptance to them. In Jesus' name, amen.

Keep This Close

As you go on your way this week, here are some thoughts that you may want to save in your phone or write on a sticky note so you can refer back to them:

- Freedom is any place in us that believes we are fully and finally accepted in God.
- He has sent me to proclaim liberty to the captives, and recovering of sight to the blind. (Luke 4:18)

SESSION 2

On Your Own

Memory Verse

This week, continue to practice saying aloud your memory verse:

She gave this name to the LORD who spoke to her:
"You are the God who sees me."

(GENESIS 16:13 NIV)

In Real Life:

DRAMA ACTIVITY: Cut and Run

In the drama, a woman reflected on her life while knitting. She realized looking back that she was a person who simply cut the yarn when things got tangled up. In other words, she ran away. She has come to see the value in a long skein of yarn.

1 How would you describe your life in terms of knitting? For instance, is your life like one big ball of yarn that can be used for a whole project? Is it cut up into pieces? Is it a tangled mess, or have you worked to untangle portions of it?

2 Have you ever run away from someone or something? What have been the consequences of your running away, or not running away?

3 If God were to knit your life into one harmonious whole, what are some of the pieces you would like him to draw together?

4 Read Luke 15:11–32. This is Jesus' great story about a young man who runs away. Or is it? In truth, both young men run away from their father in different ways. How does each son run away from his father?

5 What does the father do about each son's choice to run away from him?

6 The younger son eventually decides to go home. What does the father's response to him say about the father?

7 We aren't told whether the older son ever decides to truly go home to his father. How does this affect what you take away from the story?

8 Which son are you more like? How? What would going home to the father look like in your life today?

Hagar in the Bible

SCRIPTURE ACTIVITY

Look up Genesis 16:7–16 and reread this part of Hagar's story.

When we last saw Hagar, she was running away from Sarah after Sarah abused her. Hagar is pregnant. She is Egyptian, so naturally she flees in the direction of Egypt. But between her and Egypt is the vast Sinai desert. She gets as far as a spring many days into the desert when the angel of the Lord speaks to her.

1. If you were alone and pregnant in the middle of a desert, who could you call? What would you post on social media?

2. In verse 8, the angel asks Hagar a question, and she doesn't fully answer it. She says where she has come from, but she doesn't say where she is going. That says a lot about her situation.

3. Consider what the angel says in verse 9. How do you think the angel's words affect Hagar? Why?

4 Would you be encouraged by the angel's words in verses 10-12? Why or why not?

5 God's instruction to Hagar may seem harsh, but she was in a situation with no good options. She was a pregnant woman in the desert, vulnerable to heat, hunger, thirst, wild animals, and abuse by nomadic traders. Going back to Abraham and Sarah may have been her only choice for survival.

6 Think about how Hagar responds to the angel's words in verse 13. What do her words say about how the angel's words have affected her?

7 Why do you think she feels that God has seen her?

8 Do you feel that God has seen you? Why or why not?

9 God doesn't make new circumstances possible for Hagar at this point. She has to go back to Abraham and Sarah. How does that make you feel about God? Why?

Fear of rejection allows men to have the power only GOD should.

Journal Time

Choose one of the following topics to journal about:

- Are you finally and fully accepted in Jesus? Do you truly believe him when he says you are? What in your life suggests that you do believe him? What in your life suggests that you don't? What helps you believe him? What gets in the way? Who could help you get past the events you have experienced that tell you there are things you have to do to earn acceptance?
- What are the things you have done or are doing that make you wonder whether you have disqualified yourself from God's full acceptance? Give some thought to your past, and identify those things that make you think, "Nope, God can't accept me with that." Then give some focused thought to your actions and habits now, and see if there is anything that makes you think, "No, it is too much for God to love me while I'm doing that."
- Reflect on one of the destructive things you have done. Let God ask you, "What's wrong?" Let him ask you gently and lovingly, "Why did you do that?" Where in your heart had you gone to get to the place where you did that?
- What are some of the things you have done, or that you do now, to try to earn love from God or another person? What have been the consequences of those actions? How do they affect you? How do they affect other people? How do they affect the way you relate to God?
- What are you scared of? Are you scared of your honest story? Of being vulnerable? Of stepping out into something new and unknown? Of just being a regular woman? Are you scared of the rejection that might happen to you if you take action?

Whichever topic(s) you choose, finish by answering this question: What will I choose to do differently in my day-to-day life as a result of this reflection? Use extra paper if necessary.

TEACHING ACTIVITY

We can push memories of rejection deep into our subconscious and never deal with them. Over time, they fracture us, inside and outside. They can keep us from having really meaningful relationships.

Think back over your past from your earliest memories, through your time at school, until now. When did you experience rejection? When were you not fully accepted on your worst days? When did you think you needed to earn someone's love?

Choose one of those memories, and using the space provided, describe:

- The person or people who didn't accept you
- What they did to send a rejecting message
- Where you were
- Anyone else who was involved or looking on
- How this affected your life: your growth; your hurt; your isolation; your feelings of anxiety, fear, shame, anger, numbness; your understanding of yourself; your understanding of God
- What is your part now? Where do you need to take ownership, make amends, reach out, forgive?
- How can you use this part of your past to glorify God and do good to others in the future?

PRAYER ACTIVITY

Do you have trouble embracing the truth that God accepts you even on your worst days? If so, take some time to pray over Romans 8:33–34 below:

Who will bring any charge against those whom God has chosen? It is God who justifies. Who then is the one who condemns? No one. Christ Jesus who died—more than that, who was raised to life—is at the right hand of God and is also interceding for us. (NIV)

Give yourself at least ten minutes to write a prayer about this passage. Talk with God about how you know he has chosen you, or why you're not sure. Tell him about any people from your present or your past whose voices bringing charges against you seem to resonate in your head a lot. Where are those voices of condemnation coming from? What do you think Jesus says about them? Ask him to show you why it matters that he died and was raised to life. Thank Jesus that he is interceding for you. Ask God to help you truly believe that he accepts you. Pour out your thoughts and feelings to him, the whole story that maybe you normally hold back because you're not sure if he can deal with it.

SESSION 3

Trusting After betrayal

Hagar was exploited by people in authority, people who were followers of God. This happens with tragic frequency. It may have even happened to you. Authority figures, churchgoers, and even church leaders are imperfect and sometimes shockingly selfish. When they fail to treat others with love and respect, those who are mistreated often conclude that the people of God can't be trusted. Some, indeed, cannot be. But if we make this a blanket statement about all of God's people, it is easy to cut ourselves off from the healing partnership God promises through a faith community. In fact, the more distance we put between ourselves and those empowered by the Holy Spirit, the less we experience and acknowledge God's work. We may even be distanced from God as we distance ourselves from God's people.

If this describes you, if you have been hiding out at the margins of a church community because you've been burned, or if you have been avoiding church altogether, don't give up. Hagar shows us that an awful situation like this can be redeemed. Whether you have been harmed by people in the church or out of the church, God can restore you to a place where you can feel safe being in partnership with people again. In this study we will consider how healing happens, how to build a healthy church community, and what forgiveness is and isn't. You aren't stuck with your hurts. God can bring good to a tragic story in ways that you may never have expected.

Check In

Before you dive into the video, take a few minutes to check in with each other. Give everyone a chance to respond to one of the following:

- ➔ What did you get out of the "On Your Own" practices you did for Session 2?
- ➔ When someone wrongs you or hurts you, how do you typically respond? (You can choose more than one answer or come up with your own.)

  ____ I express anger at them.
  ____ I let it go.
  ____ I hold a grudge.
  ____ Other (name it):
  ____ I withdraw.

Next, say your memory verse aloud together. Be sure to say the verse reference with it.

At a Glance: HAGAR

Age-old problem: Betrayal by followers of God

Age-old mistake: Distancing yourself from other people and refusing to trust

God's timeless wisdom: Put your trust in God, and learn from him to treat other people with love even if they're not trustworthy. *"O my God, in you I trust; let me not be put to shame; let not my enemies exult over me" (Psalm 25:2 ESV). "But love your enemies, and do good, and lend, expecting nothing in return, and your reward will be great, and you will be sons of the Most High, for he is kind to the ungrateful and the evil. Be merciful, even as your Father is merciful" (Luke 6:35–36 ESV).*

Play the video segment for Session 3. It's about 18 minutes long. As you watch, use the following outline to record thoughts that stand out to you.

DRAMA: Nicole

God can't always get you out, but he will sit right with you.

You're right where you're supposed to be. And you're not alone. God is right here with you. And that's better than out.

TEACHING: Jada

Some people have trust issues because they have been hurt by people in authority, including in the church.

You were created in the image of God. Regardless of how anyone has treated you.

A huge part of trusting God is understanding what's hurting your heart, doing the hard work, and making the choice to let it go.

You can't be used greatly by God when all of your energy is hugging tightly the things that have hurt you.

Find the community you need to be in so you can find healing.

Being hurt by God's people isn't the same as being hurt by GOD.

Group Discussion

Leader, read each numbered prompt to the group:

1. What stood out to you most from the video?

2. Jada talked about how many people she has known who have been hurt by those in authority, especially in the church. What do you think it is about churches that makes this scenario all too common?

3. Jada says, however, that the solution is not for us to avoid churches. What's wrong with this as a solution? What do we lose when we avoid churches, or when we just duck in, attend the service, and then duck out again without getting involved?

4. What can we do to make church a safe and healthy place for people to get involved? How can we contribute?

5 How do you think a person can heal after she has suffered a violation of her trust? What does she need to do? What help does she need from people? What help does she need from God?

Select a volunteer

to read the following:

Jada talked about the importance of understanding what is hurting our hearts. Burying the hurt won't help us truly move on. Rehearsing our resentment over and over won't help us move on either. We need to come to understand what happened to us, why it hurts so much, and how it is still affecting us. We may need the help of a wise and trusted person, or several people, to gain this kind of understanding. It is sometimes hard to come to understand our own pain without talking about it with someone who will listen, not judge, and help us explore how it is affecting who we are now.

Jada also spoke of forgiveness, which lets go of the desire to get even or get what is fair. Forgiveness does not mean saying what the other person did to us was okay, and it doesn't mean saying the pain is insignificant. Forgiveness simply means choosing to let go of the bitterness and the desire to make others pay for what they did.

6 God asks us to forgive those who have harmed us. Why do you suppose this is often so hard for us to do?

7 How does knowing that you were created in God's image and that you are his help you deal with the ways you have been hurt?

In preparation for the coming week, write one thing you want to gain from your study time:

(ex: hope for my future, a better understanding of who I am . . .)

Closing Prayer

Ask a volunteer to read this prayer aloud over the group:

God of heaven and earth, you are the one in charge of justice, of allowing people to face the consequences of their wrong actions. We want to let go of the hurt that has come from the people who have harmed us. Help us lay down our desire to see that they "get what they deserve," knowing that there have been times by your grace that we have not had to suffer what we deserve. We offer these hurts to you, these people to you, and we ask your help in truly entrusting them to *your* justice, believing you will help our feelings catch up to our choice. We also ask you to heal our broken ability to trust and enable us to enter into relationships going forward where we can be honest, vulnerable, and safe. Thank you that you are with us. You have climbed into the backseat to comfort us in our pain and you will never leave us. We are yours, always and forever. In Jesus' name, amen.

Keep This Close

As you go on your way this week, here are some thoughts that you may want to save in your phone or write on a sticky note so you can refer back to them.

- You are not alone in your pain. I am right here with you. And my presence is better than out.
- I am created in the image of God. Regardless of how anyone has treated me, I am still his.
- Don't be overcome by evil, but overcome evil with good.

SESSION 3

On Your Own

Memory Verse

This week, continue to practice saying aloud your memory verse:

She gave this name to the LORD who spoke to her: "You are the God who sees me."

(GENESIS 16:13 NIV)

In Real Life:

DRAMA ACTIVITY: Out, Out, OUT

A businesswoman sits in her car and remembers a time twenty years ago when her son was small and God spoke to her through a situation in a car.

1 Have you ever just wanted out of a situation? If so, what was it about that situation that made out seem like the only viable solution?

2 Why didn't the woman in the drama get her son out of the car? Do you think she should have or not? Looking back at your own situation, were there factors that now make sense that explain why you couldn't just get out?

3 Maybe you were able to get out of your tough situation. If so, how were the results satisfying or not satisfying? If not, what were the results of staying in?

4 What if God said to you right now, “You’re right where you’re supposed to be. And you’re not alone. I am right here with you. And that’s better than out”? Does having God with you in your current situation feel like it is enough for you? Why or why not?

5 What do you think it means to have God “with you” in a situation? What does he do and not do? (If it’s helpful, you can look at John 14:16–17, 26–27.)

There are things about modern Western culture that make it harder for us to be aware of God with us. In a world inundated with artificial connections and online relationships, it is easy to think of ourselves as separate, at a distance from everything we think of as outside ourselves. For example, we think of our minds as separate from our bodies. An illness can happen to the body and we say,

"I'm not letting it get to me," as if "me" is separate from "my body." We also think of ourselves as separate from the people around us. What happens to them doesn't necessarily affect our sense of well-being. Thus, we don't relate to a feeling common in the ancient world and still common in Asian cultures today: the feeling of shame because someone in our family has brought shame on the family. In the West we think our family isn't "us." In the same way, we don't relate to the idea that we need to be part of a church family because God wants to relate to us as a community, not only as individuals. Many of us just want to experience God one-on-one. "Forget community, forget the body of Christ, just me and Jesus is all I need." But when we distance ourselves from our own bodies, from other people, from "the world" and the church, we inevitably hold God at a distance too. We think he's the one being distant, when in fact, it's us.

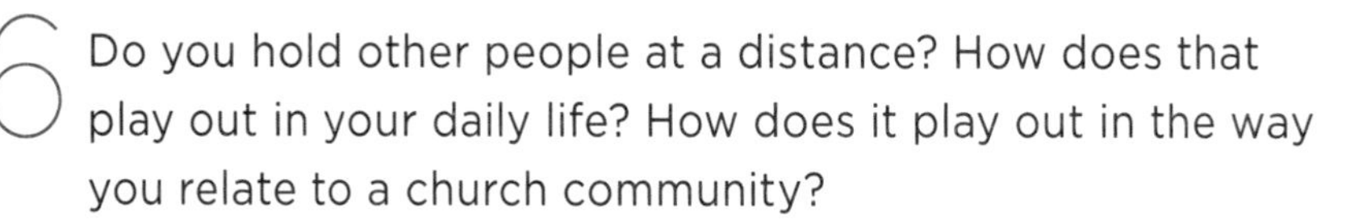

6 Do you hold other people at a distance? How does that play out in your daily life? How does it play out in the way you relate to a church community?

7 Do you think you hold God at a distance? What makes you think you do or you don't?

8 Spend some time praying through Psalm 46. Write down 2–3 things the psalm says to you about God's presence with you.

WHEN life does not **affirm** your *significance*, **God will.**

Authority Figures

TEACHING ACTIVITY

Have you been hurt by someone in authority, in the church or elsewhere? If so, this exercise gives you a chance to process that experience and move into healing. Think about the person or people who hurt you. Write about the following:

What place of authority or position did they hold in your life?

____

What did they do to hurt you or betray your trust? ________

____

Was there anyone else who was involved or aware of what was going on? If so, who? ______________________

____

How has this affected your life: your growth; your hurt; your isolation; your feelings of anxiety, fear, shame, anger, numbness; your understanding of yourself; your understanding of God? Have you grieved this hurt? Tell God how this made you feel. Ask God how it made him feel.

What is your part now? Where do you need to take ownership, make amends, reach out, forgive? Even if you feel that others were 99% to blame, is there 1% you can give toward reconciliation in heart? Reconciliation in person is ideal, but if that's not possible, can you do the work of forgiving with a friend or counselor, with the help of God's grace?

Do you resist doing your part now? If so, what is that voice of resistance inside you saying?

How can you use this part of your past to glorify God and do good to others in the future?

SCRIPTURE ACTIVITY

Look up Genesis 17:1-26 and read it.

Hagar was pregnant with Ishmael when she ran away. But after her encounter with the God who sees, she returned a different woman to Abraham and Sarah's household. When we next pick up the story, Hagar's son Ishmael is thirteen years old (Genesis 17:25). Many years have passed in the household of Abraham, Sarah, Hagar, and Ishmael. We're not told how the four of them got along.

1. The Bible doesn't tell us about those formative years for Hagar and Ishmael. What do you imagine life was like for Hagar as a slave in Sarah's household and as the mother of Abraham's son for those fourteen years? What might have been the hard parts? Any good parts?

2. What kind of father might Abraham have been to Ishmael? How might that have affected his relationship with Sarah?

3 Read Genesis 17:15–21 again. What does God promise for Sarah here? How will her life change when this happens?

4 How will this affect the now-teenage Ishmael?

5 How will Hagar's life be affected when Sarah gets pregnant?

6 Sarah chose to use Hagar as a surrogate mother and Abraham agreed. Neither this plan nor the consequences involved God's promise. Now, years later, God is fulfilling his promise to Abraham and giving him a son through Sarah. He doesn't choose Ishmael to inherit the promise; he chooses Isaac. What does this situation tell us about God? About human nature?

7 If you were Hagar, what would you say to God when you get the news that Sarah is pregnant? How would God's promise in verse 20 affect, or not affect, what you say?

REFLECTION ACTIVITY

Merriam-Webster's top definition of forgiveness for English language learners is "to stop feeling anger toward (someone who has done something wrong)." But this is not what the Bible means by forgiveness. In the Bible, forgiveness is a choice, and you can't choose to stop feeling a feeling. Rather, your feelings will change (perhaps over time) in response to the choices you make.

There are other misunderstandings of forgiveness that we should clear out of the way. First, forgiveness does not require you to forget the offense. You can't choose to forget. But unless you forgive, the memory stays intact and can be triggered years later at the same intensity. Time is not a healer; God is. He wants us to remember his faithfulness to us time and again until we know he is enough.

Second, forgiveness does not require you to deny that what happened was wrong or that you were deeply hurt. To the contrary, to begin the process of forgiveness one must give words to the offense, be shocked and angry at evil, and not rationalize it away. Third, you don't have to accept excuses for the other person's behavior.

Also, forgiveness doesn't ask you to trust the other person again. If the person has a pattern of wrong behavior, you should put boundaries around your relationship with her. If the other person establishes a new pattern of behavior, you can then choose to rebuild trust over time.

So if forgiveness doesn't ask all that of you, what does it ask? First of all, it asks you to let go of the demand that the other person pay for what she did. You renounce the desire for equal harm to come to the other person. You even renounce the demand for fairness. You accept that you have borne the high price for the wrongdoing by others, and you're not going to demand compensation. (If the person did something illegal, that's a separate issue. We're talking about interpersonal relationships.)

Second, forgiveness asks you to treat the other person with love. You may not have warm feelings toward her right away, but love means you *actively seek her good.* You look for opportunities to treat her with kindness and respect. You ask God to show you what will build her up, and you act on that insight. Feelings of compassion may follow your choice to act. If you're no longer in a relationship with the person, you can actively seek her good by praying for her and never speaking of her in a negative way.

The real fruit of forgiveness is that it allows us to approach new relationships with openness and love. When one person betrays our trust, it is easy to decide to stop trusting altogether. But forgiveness frees us from that stance. It moves us toward trustworthy people and gives them a chance to be part of our healing.

Forgiveness is good for us. When we hold onto resentment, it harms us much more than it harms the other person. We are the ones who stay stuck, when we could be living in freedom and love instead.

Forgiveness is often a process more than a one-time event. The questions in this section may only begin that process. They are intended to help you identify where you are getting stuck in forgiving.

The process of forgiveness often begins as you express your anger and hurt to God, perhaps in writing, and perhaps to another person as well. For example, what is the experience that you are struggling to forgive? What happened? What are you feeling? You may want to use the questions listed above under "Authority Figures" to process the events and how they have affected you. If you are ready to go to the next step, then the questions in this exercise may be helpful to you.

1 What is holding you back from forgiving someone? Write down all your questions and reservations.

2 Do you resent God for allowing this person to hurt you? Describe your feelings toward God.

3 Read Matthew 18:21–35. A “talent” (verse 24) is a unit of money worth about twenty year’s wages for a laborer. A denarius (verse 28) is worth one day’s wage. What reason does this story give for why we should keep forgiving our brothers and sisters over and over?

4 Deep down, do you buy the claim that you owe God ten thousand talents’ worth of debt? Take some time to write about how you have or haven’t wronged God. Think about the fact that he created the universe, and everything in it belongs to him. Think about the fact that he made you, and he consistently gives you food and water and shelter

no matter what your behavior is. Have you had a consistent attitude of thankfulness and respect for him, or have you taken his generosity for granted, like you might deserve it? Have you consistently acknowledged his right to be in charge of your life, or have you tried to take control? Do you seek to follow his agenda or your own? Do you treat His people as Jesus treated them? (Do questions like these make you feel attacked or humbled?)

5 After reflecting on what you owe God, are you persuaded that he has forgiven you for more than what this other person owes you? Why or why not?

6 What will it cost you if you forgive the person who hurt you?

7 What will it cost you if you choose not to forgive?

PRAYER ACTIVITY

Write a letter to God about a hurt you have suffered because of someone else. Pour out your heart to him. He really wants to hear what's on your heart. If it's helpful, read Psalm 55. Use your private journal if you prefer.

Now write God's response. If you like, check out Psalm 34:18 and Luke 6:27-36.

SESSION 4

Transformed and Seen

Have you ever felt invisible or insignificant in comparison with others? Perhaps you were the "good kid" in your family or classroom, where the troublemakers got all the attention. Maybe you've never fit in with the athletes, creatives, or intellectuals. Maybe your life feels less than Instagram-post worthy. Perhaps you've attended more weddings as a bridesmaid than years you've been alive and wonder when it will be your turn.

As a woman and a slave, Hagar was invisible in her culture. Yet when her life bottomed out, God spoke to her, and she realized God had seen her. That moment transformed her life. Being seen by God changed Hagar. Her circumstances were still far from ideal, yet she was able to handle them because she knew she was seen by a power greater than her circumstances. In this final study, we will explore what it means to be seen by God and how that affects the way we deal with an unknown future.

Check In

Before you dive into the video, take a few minutes to check in with each other. Let each person choose one of the following to respond to:

- What did you get out of the "On Your Own" practices you did for Session 3?
- If you could have God's full attention, what is one thing you would like to say to him?

Next, say your memory verse aloud together, along with its reference.

At a Glance: HAGAR

Age-old problem: Feeling insignificant

Age-old mistake: Overcompensating in word or deed to get attention

God's timeless wisdom: Rest, and respond in love, trusting that God sees you. Waiting and responding and trusting can be difficult. But God doesn't just see our external circumstances, he knows what is going on inside our hearts as well. *"O Lord, you have searched me and known me! You know when I sit down and when I rise up; you discern my thoughts from afar" (Psalm 139:1–2 ESV).*

Video Notes

Play the video segment for Session 4. It's about 28 minutes long, and you will be introduced to three speakers. As you watch, use the following outline to record thoughts that stand out to you.

DRAMA: Nicole

I don't care what the owners think, I care what you think. I care what Katie thinks, and she's proud of me.

TEACHING: Kasey

God sees Hagar just because he wants to.

Hagar knows she is free, regardless of what does or does not change in her external circumstance.

Where are you hiding out? Where are you fearful? God sees you. Draw near.

TEACHING: *Jada*

Nothing you do, good or bad, surprises God or makes him love you less.

When you mess up, that's when you draw near to him.

The answer is him. It's his presence. That alone is enough.

Group Discussion

Leader, read each numbered to the group.

1 In the drama, the diner manager says that ultimately, she doesn't care what the diner owners think of her. She cares what God thinks and what her daughter thinks.

Whose opinion matters to you? Whose opinion actually affects what you do and how you feel about yourself? Is there a difference between the audience you're playing to and the audience you think you *should* be playing to?

Select a volunteer

to read the following:

Hagar says to God, "You are the God who sees me." What does it mean to be seen by God? First, it means that the God who runs the universe notices us. He pays attention to us. We matter. Second, it means that he knows everything about us. We often don't see our past or our present as they really are, and we're completely blind to our future. God, on the other hand, sees the whole of our life through the lens of his sovereignty. He sees our strengths and weaknesses. He sees our virtues and faults. He sees the good and the bad, and he never turns away. He turns toward us in love. Third, it means he cares about our pain and our needs. He grieves with us when we feel scared or rejected. Fourth, it means he provides what we need (although not everything we want) to be at peace despite the painful circumstance or hurtful person. Finally, and most importantly, being seen by God means he gives us the opportunity to experience him and be satisfied by him, who is more beautiful and desirable than anything in our universe.

2 What difference does it make to your life whether or not God sees you? Does it make any difference in what you do?

3 Kasey said the moment Hagar knew God saw her was the moment she was free inside, regardless of what did or didn't change about her external circumstance. Why do you think being seen has that effect?

4 God is right here, willing to grieve with us through the hard things of life. How do we take advantage of that offer?

5 Many people are unaware that God sees them. What do you think gets in the way of that awareness?

6 Jada said, "When you delight in the Lord, the Lord will deliver and rescue." What does it mean to delight in the Lord?

7 Take a minute on your own and write down your response to this question (you won't have to share your answer): On a scale of 0 to 5, how confident are you that you totally belong to God despite your popularity or platform in the world? Mark where you are on the measuring line below.

0	1	2	3	4	5
Not at all confident					Very confident

Has anything changed for you since Session 1? If so, what?

8 Now share with the group: What are you grateful for that you've received from this study on Hagar? What will you take with you?

In preparation for the coming week, write one thing you want to gain from your study time:

(ex: hope for my future, a better understanding of who I am . . .)

Closing Prayer

Ask a volunteer to read this prayer over the group:

Creator God, thank you that you see us. Thank you that we matter to you, that you grieve with us, that you provide for us. Thank you that you know us completely and still accept us. We want to take you up on your offer to know you as much as an infinite and infinitely desirable God can be known. We entrust our circumstances into your hands, and we ask you to care for our needs as you see best. And most of all, we ask for the awareness that your Presence goes with us, because you are our hearts' desire. In Jesus' name, amen.

Keep This Close

As you go on your way this week and end this study, here are some thoughts that you may want to save in your phone or write on a sticky note so you can refer back to them and remember them.

- → You see me in my pain and you grieve with me.
- → I never have to hide from God.
- → When I delight in the Lord, he will deliver and rescue.

SESSION 4

On Your Own

Memory Verse

Continue to practice saying aloud your memory verse:

She gave this name to the LORD who spoke to her: You are the God who sees me."

(GENESIS 16:13 NIV)

In Real Life:

DRAMA ACTIVITY: Enough, Part 2

The diner manager returns with a new perspective because she has learned that her daughter is proud of her. She says she cares about what her daughter thinks of her and what God thinks.

1. Think to yourself about what the following say about the audiences you are performing for and how much you care about what they think:
   - The way you present yourself and treat people when you are at work. (Take a few minutes to cast your mind back to the last time you were at work and how you acted throughout the workday. If your work takes place at home, you can either answer accordingly or skip this item.)
   - The way you present yourself and treat people when you are with family. (Again, take a few minutes to picture some scenes with your family.)
   - The way you present yourself and treat people when you are at church
   - The way you behave, treat people, treat responsibilities when no one can see you except God

2 Who do you think God sees when he looks at you?

______________________________________.

3 Read Psalm 139. Then focus on verses 1–6. Do you like being seen by God in this way?

What are the plusses?

What are the minuses?

4 Consider what the psalmist says about hiding in verses 7–12. Are you glad that God is there, whether you go to exalted places or dark places? Or does that give you some discomfort? Why?

5 How does knowing God sees you affect the importance you attach to whether others see you? How does it affect your concern for what they think of you? What would it look like to live for an audience of One?

Hagar in the Bible

SCRIPTURE ACTIVITY

Read Genesis 21.

Ishmael was thirteen years old when God promised that Sarah would have a son the following year. So he was fourteen when Isaac was born, as Genesis 21:1–7 recounts. Then the story skips ahead to when Isaac was weaned (verse 8) at about age three. So that makes Ishmael about seventeen. He was not a tiny child and knew full well what was going on. And Hagar was no longer a young woman.

1. Abraham doesn't want to do what Sarah asks in verse 10, but God tells him to do it (verses 11–13). How might this be better for Hagar and Ishmael in the long run?

2. In the short run, though, it is very hard on Hagar and Ishmael. They go out into the semi-desert and run out of water. Ishmael gets faint from dehydration, and Hagar has to half-carry, half-drag him into the shade of a bush (verse 15). Then she goes far enough away that she doesn't have to watch him die, and she starts to weep loudly.

3 Have you ever been in a situation when you felt like that? If so, when? What did you do?

4 The name "Ishmael" means "God heard." The name appears nowhere in this chapter, but verse 17 begins with the same syllables: "God heard." This highlights the importance of the words. Why does it matter that God heard?

GOD is saying, "I see you, I know, and I'm with you. I am El Roi. Nothing catches me by *surprise*."

5 Consider what God does when he hears (verses 17–21). Do you believe God hears you like that? What helps you believe that? Or what gets in the way?

6 Ishmael wasn't the chosen son, the son of the promise. He was the son who was sent away, the son of a slave. And yet, verse 20 insists, "God was with the boy." Do you think that makes up for the rejection? Why or why not?

7 How do you respond to the way Hagar's story is left at the end? What are your thoughts and feelings?

8 What will you take away from the story of Hagar? What has it told you about God? About yourself? About life?

Journal Time

Choose one of the following topics to journal about:

- Jada said, "When you mess up, that's when you draw near to God. That's when you go to church, that's when you call for prayer. That's when you let your friends know what's going on. God never wants us to hide from him." Do you do these things when you mess up, or do you hide? What motivates you to do what you do? How helpful is what you do? If you face obstacles in doing what Jada recommends, how might you address those obstacles?
- Jada said, "Very often, we think that when God seeks us out, he's going to give us the answer we've been waiting for. But the truth is, the answer is him. It's his presence. That alone is enough." Is God's presence enough for you? Why or why not? How do you think we know when God's presence is with us? Is his presence with you? How important is intimacy with God to you, compared with the other things you want?
- What do you think it means to delight in God? What sorts of attitudes and behaviors do you think it involves? Do you delight in God? Why do you or don't you? How does delighting in God (or not delighting in him) affect your life?
- In Session 2 you thought about whether you believe God accepts you completely or whether you believe there are things you have to do to earn love. Where are you now with that? How has your study of Hagar helped you, or not helped you, with that?

Whichever option you choose, finish by answering this question: What do I want to do differently in my day-to-day life as a result of this reflection?

PRAYER ACTIVITY

Take some time to talk with God about delighting in him. What are some reasons you have for delighting in him? Tell him those. Then tell him about the things in your life that have been barriers to delight. You might talk with him about things you reflected on earlier in this study, such as ways people have hurt you, times you've felt rejected, shame and hiding, or feeling that you need to earn love. Tell him how much you need him to heal you in the place of your hurts and put you on a fresh path. Ask him to help you know that he fully accepts you as you are. Ask him to help you delight in him in the midst of whatever has happened to you in the past and whatever is going on in your life now. If it's helpful, write your prayer here.

Now, what do you think God might want to say in response? See, for example, Romans 9:25–26; Ephesians 5:1–2; Song of Solomon 2:8–15.

About the Authors

Jada Edwards, Bible Teacher, Speaker, Author

Jada is an experienced Bible teacher and has committed her life to equipping women of all ages with practical, biblical truth. She currently serves as the Women's Pastor and as the Director of Creative Services for One Community Church in Plano, Texas. Jada teaches a midweek women's Bible study to over 1,300 women each week. She has authored two books based on her Bible studies: *Captive Mind* and *Thirst*. She and her husband, Conway, have a son, Joah, and a daughter, Chloe.

Nicole Johnson, Dramatist and Author

A bestselling author, performer, and motivational speaker, Nicole is one of the most sought-after creative communicators in America today. Her unique ability to blend humor with compassion, as she captures the inner-most feelings of women facing life's daily struggles, has enabled her to create a unique sense of community for women of all ages. Nicole has 20 years' experience as an actor, television host, and producer, and has published eight books and a variety of curricula regarding relationships. She has written and performed sketches for the Women of Faith Conferences and written and directed dramas for The Revolve Tour. For three years, she wrote and performed dramatic sketches with relationship expert Dr. Gary Smalley, bringing her unique perspective to his seminars.

Kasey Van Norman, Author, Bible Teacher, Counselor

Kasey is a bestselling author, licensed counselor, and Bible teacher living in Bryan, Texas with her husband, Justin, and their two children, Emma Grace and Lake. Kasey has published two books with Bible studies, *Named by God* and *Raw Faith*. Kasey teaches and writes about the love that redeemed her life from the shame of past abuse, addiction, infidelity, and the fear of a life-threatening cancer diagnosis. She teaches thousands of women each year as a ministry event speaker—a headliner with the Extraordinary Women Conferences and American Association of Christian Counselors, and as an ambassador with Compassion International.

The women in the Bible asked the same three questions we all still ask today:

How does everyone else see me?

How do I see myself?

How does God see me?

The Known by Name series explores complex women in the Bible and their struggles with tough questions through the lenses of a counselor, a Bible teacher, and a dramatist.

Kasey Van Norman is a bestselling author, licensed counselor, and Bible teacher living in Texas with her husband and their two children. Kasey teaches and writes about the love that redeemed her life from the shame of past abuse, addiction, infidelity, and the fear of a life-threatening cancer diagnosis.

Jada Edwards is an experienced Bible teacher committed to equipping women of all ages with practical, biblical truth. She currently serves as the Women's Pastor and Director of Creative Services for One Community Church in Plano, Texas. She and her husband have two children.

Nicole Johnson, bestselling author, performer, and motivational speaker, is one of the most sought-after creative communicators in America today. She uniquely blends humor with compassion, creating a sense of community for women of all ages. She makes California home with her husband and children.

RAHAB

Don't Judge Me,
God Says I'm

Qualified

Rahab's story, found in the book of Joshua, is a story of a girl boss, an assertive, confident woman who did what she had to do to provide for her family. Her identity was shaped by her upbringing. With no Bible study to join or podcast to download, Rahab learned her behaviors in a culture that believed in gods, not God. But when opportunity knocked, she boldly trusted in God, and became a woman who brought freedom to generations.

This four-session video Bible study will take you through the story of Rahab, our sister in Scripture who trusted God's final word about her worth above society's. Through her story, you will learn how to shed unhelpful labels and fears, and instead revel in God's unconditional love and acceptance of you—just as you are.

HAGAR

In the Face of Rejection,
God Says I'm

Significant

Hagar's story, found in Genesis 16, is a story of cultural victimization. She was betrayed, abandoned, and scorned. Her response? She did what most of us would do when deeply hurt by someone we trust—she ran away. She got defensive. She retreated to a place where she felt safe. She felt justified in her anger and hurt. But deep in her core was a woman who longed to be seen and hoped for redemption.

This four-session video Bible study will take you through the story of Hagar, our sister in Scripture who learns through hurt and rejection that what is unresolved is not unseen by God. Through her story, you will learn how to respond when life doesn't affirm you, but God does.

NAOMI

When I Feel Worthless,
God Says I'm

Enough

Naomi's story, found in the book of Ruth, is a story of lost identity. She lost her husband and her sons, which in her culture left her completely without a home or a means to support herself. She was a Hebrew woman in Moabite territory, alone among strangers. She reacted by letting her circumstances define her. But even in her angry, fearful, rather dramatic season of feeling like the victim, God kept showing his faithfulness.

This four-session video Bible study will take you through the story of Naomi, our sister in Scripture who traveled from comfort and security to despair and bitterness; from hopeless drifting to faithful obedience; from loss to redemption in one short lifetime.

Available now at your favorite bookstore.